WHEN POEMS FALL FROM THE SKY

in association with the Royal Botanic Gardens, Kew

Royal Botanic Gardens **Kew**

About the Royal Botanic Gardens, Kew

The Royal Botanic Gardens Kew is a world famous scientific organization and home to two elegant gardens in the South East of England—Kew Gardens in South West London and Wakehurst in West Sussex which also houses Kew's Millennium Seed Bank. Kew Gardens is a recognized World Heritage Site, with stunning greenhouses and a rich history of royal heritage interwoven with the development of modern day plant science and sustainable development.

Your purchase supports the vital work of Kew—saving the plants and fungi around the world that might one day save us.

For my grandchildren, Joseph, Fiona, and Arlo

Published in 2022 by Welbeck Editions
An Imprint of Welbeck Children's Limited,
part of Welbeck Publishing Group.
Based in London and Sydney. www.welbeckpublishing.com

First published in 2021 by ZaZa Kids Books.

ISBN 978 1 80338 059 9

Designed by Sarah Pyke

Printed in Dongguan, China

10 9 8 7 6 5 4 3 2 1

FSC
www.fsc.org

MIX
Paper | Supporting
responsible forestry
FSC® C144853

WHEN POEMS FALL FROM THE SKY

Zaro Weil

illustrated by Junli Song

WELBECK
EDITIONS

STORY OF THIS BOOK

When I was young I imagined the sun rose the instant I opened my eyes in the morning. It was simple. I asked it to. And at night I was sure that a thousand twinkling stars popped out the moment I blinked and looked up.

I believed with all my heart that I shared something personal with nature. With the sun, moon, stars, plants, creatures, mountains, river, sea, and everything else on and around the planet. That in some unexplained way we could all talk together. Maybe not in human words. But through strong, almost magical feelings of communication.

My secret was that if I listened hard enough, looked long and wide, and felt deep enough inside, the world would share its stories with me.

That idea quietly grew over the years. Of course, I never mentioned it to anyone.

Then not long ago I decided to spend the whole day in one of my favorite places, Kew Gardens, in London. Walking along, I spotted spring gum-drop flowers and smiled at the exuberant trees in all shapes and descriptions. I heard bird sounds and followed tiny sun glints as they fell onto a million shades of green spreading and twining inside the crystal-clear greenhouses.

I kept going. Before long my imagination sat up and took note. Kew began to talk to me. The garden introduced me to the quiet spaces between the trees. Welcomed me to webs of eerie, inky afternoon shadows. I heard silence ripen in the long stretches of grass and smelled deep-down earth pulsing its wild mysteries under my feet.

By the end of the afternoon, as the sun slow-slid away, I saw things differently.

Felt different.

The garden had shared a secret or two with me.

And that's how the idea for this book was born. A book where nature and its creatures shared its secrets, its stories with us.

In my version nature talks in poems.

Poems that fall, in an enchanted blink, from the sky . . . when nothing is as it seems and everything appears as it just might be.

And as you turn these pages you'll discover that nature is sharing with you its deepest mysteries, timeless stories, and forever-after songs of hope.

STORY OF THANKS

I thank my lucky stars every day for getting to meet Junli Song. She has been always brilliant and heartfelt; endowing my words with new sensibilities through her breathtaking art.

Judith Elliott has been my beloved mentor, brilliant advisor, and great friend for a very long time. She has firmly guided and helped shape every word, line, and thought inside this book.

Enormous appreciation to the wonderful team at Welbeck Editions and to our designer Sarah Pyke.

Gina Fullerlove and Lydia White, from Royal Botanic Gardens, Kew, have been supportive and enthusiastic. Indeed, it was Gina's eye-opening tour of the great Herbarium at Kew that inspired the poem-story in this book, *The Magic House of Seeds*.

I would also like to note those friends who have quietly read these poems and offered insightful comments; Jane O. Wayne and Georg Patzer.

Lisa Dempsey has generously helped me with all things electronic.

A special note of appreciation to CLPE, that wonderful organization devoted to literacy in primary education, who had the kindness to award Junli and me their prestigious CLiPPA poetry prize for our last book, CHERRY MOON.

Finally, biggest thanks to family, friends, and colleagues who, over the years, have always been by my side. Especially my husband and touchstone, Gareth Jenkins.

FOREWORD

BY MOTHER NATURE

When you think
Once upon a time
Consider me
For who else
Keeps all earth
Alive in song

When you think
Into the future
Consider yourselves
For who else
Holds all earth
In their hands

CONTENTS

THREE SUN HAIKU

crystal bright
sprinkle kind
feeding earth
you big round sugar
sky-candy

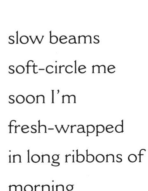

slow beams
soft-circle me
soon I'm
fresh-wrapped
in long ribbons of
morning

once gone
I think of you
please come back
like me better
than that dark cloud

AND SO IT'S SPRING

and so
it's spring
rolling over the garden
igniting pinks
summoning greens
soon everyone will
turn up
I'm absolutely
sure

DANCE WITH ME MOON

dance with me

moon

twirl me here

swing me there

turn me

twist me

in barefoot roundabouts

swirl me

faster and faster

higher and higher

till even my wobbly

earth shadow

can't keep up

BUTTERFLY'S SONG

good morning wind
remember me
I was here
just yesterday
playing with you

maybe my camouflage
fooled you
did you think
I was just some flower
or leaf
that got caught
in one of your
pushy
proud
puffs

IF YOU CAN HEAR ME

if you can hear me

know that I dream

big things for you

skies of pink

whenever you wish

snow-dust stories

whenever you hope

starry blossoms

whenever you wake

but most of all the

pit-a-pat heartbeat of

earth still green

sea still blue

ice still cold

THREE FLOWER HAIKU

flower grows from stone
but how can that be
small seed must rest
deep inside

dandelions in grass
sprout yellow
so yellow
no one sees
the green

water spills from sky

falls hard

daisy ripples

in every shade

of bright

HICKORY DICKORY MIRTH

Hickory dickory mirth
The sun's having fun with the earth
When it came to the spring
She beamed, 'Flowers, now sing
And start rhyming for all you are worth'

The flowers went singing in glee

Though all of their notes were off-key

When sun shouted, 'Encore!'

They could think of no more

So they stopped for a nice cup of tea

And when tea was all done

They resumed one by one

Just by singing their ear-tickle names

Funnier

    Rhymier

        Jolly good timier

            Wonderfurl tongue-popping games. . .

Geraniums, violets in posies
Magnolias, begonias, and rosies
Tulips, gardenias, lilies so bright
Daffodils, bluebells, and edelweiss
Columbine, poppies, anemones
Lavender, iris, and peonies

Asters and foxgloves, pink ladies' tears
Buttercups, zinnias, silver lambs' ears
Cosmos, verbena, pansies, veronica
Dandelions, nigellas, the lovely japonica

Orchids, fritillaries, butterworts, marigolds
Sunflowers, hyacinths, carnations a millionfold
Snapdragons, snowdrops, primroses, and dahlias
Crocus, camellias, hibiscus, lobelias

Rudbeckia, alyssum, clematis, and clover. . .

'STOP. . .

Oh, flowers,' sun laughs
'You're so funny, goodness me
I must catch my breath
And have a sip of that tea'

So in hickory dickory Kew
Flowers sing in every hue
Rhyming their names
In ridiculous games
Playing shadow-and-sun peek-a-boo

TELL ME SHADOW

tell me
shadow
how did you
grow so fast into that
inky tattoo
I stepped on
just
this afternoon

after all
you were nowhere
when I woke up
early this morning

think about it
shadow
everything else
takes such a
long time
to grow

apple trees
mountains
me

but not you
my guess is
you wait
hovering and sun-silent
in some black riddle
of a place

a shape-changing
bobble-dark creature
bursting to plant
yourself into the
wide-open
anything-goes
light of day…

or maybe
into the high-pitched
quiet of
moonlight
where I've seen you
tangle up tall trees
fatten up lampposts
stretch passing
silhouettes

way

up

walls

tell me
do you wait
lingering
raring to go
inside absolutely
e v e r y t h i n g

if so shadow
I have to ask
does that include

me

OH HAPPY DAY

A FIG AND WASP PLAY
(A Mother Nature Production)

FIG TREE ONE

Enters center stage. Looks at the rising sun.
Stretches his branches and smiles . . .

—

Today is here. At last. The most magical of magical days.
The most happy of happy days. The teeny tiny pinky flowers
I have inside me are perfectly ready for POLLINATION!
I have waited all year for this moment.

—

Shouts out . . .

—

Hellooo!!! Where are you? I know you're there. Come and
get it, Queen Wasp One. Today's the day! Isn't it wonderful!
Time to have some fun pollinating and party up a storm.

QUEEN WASP ONE

Heads all smiles toward Fig Tree One,
her little triangle head bobbing with joy . . .

—

Oh. Yes yes yes YES! I love this day of the year, too.
How perfect, Fig Tree One. On my way.

I've gathered so much pollen. Today I am all ready to wiggle inside your fat fig fruity self and give it to you. And lay my wonderful eggs. My head is full with delicious visions of delight. This is just too figgy figgy fabulous.

—

Fig Tree One blushes and smiles . . .

QUEEN WASP TWO

Wait! Don't forget me. I'm on my way!
I want visions of delight, too.

—

Giddy with excitement, she somersaults in the clear morning air.
Her airborne frolics accentuate her tiny wasp waist . . .

QUEEN WASP THREE

Meee three! Yippee! Here comes some super pollen.
You are too too fantastic, Fig One.

—

She dives endless figure eights displaying her beautiful
bright yellow and black stripes . . .

QUEEN WASPS 4 TO 750

And us! And us! We all want to come and share visions of delight. Look, Fig Tree One. We've got loads of different kinds of pollen! Each of us has a fabulous and glorious special kind of pollen for you. Did you ever see such variety?

—

Lots more air diving and circling and laughing and general showing off . . .

FIG TREE ONE

With an earnestly sweet and serious voice . . .

—

Whoa, everyone! Sorry, Queen Wasps Two to 750. But I don't need you. Any of you. Only Queen Wasp One is right for this job. She is my special partner. Plus she is the special and perfect size for me. You see, only Queen Wasp One can pollinate me. So no offense and I am truly sorry…but um…that's how Mother Nature works. So. I think you need to think of something else fun to do today.

QUEEN WASPS TWO to 750

What? Are you kidding? Why not, Fig Tree One?

Why not choose us?

—

Lots of buzzy sobs . . .

—

We all want to give you pollen. We all want to pollinate

the tiny little pinky red flowers you grow inside.

What does Mother Nature know anyway? Life is not fair!

We are not so sure Mother Nature is right.

—

They take off in a million unhappy Queen Wasp loop-the-loops.

But just then some nearby innocent nature-loving humans

see the angry wasps. They shout out to each other

and run very far away very fast . . .

FIG TREE ONE

Feeling awfully sorry for these other 749 Queen

Wasps. And for the poor humans who

were just out for a nice walk enjoying nature . . .

Don't be blue, wasps. Don't be angry. Here's how it is.
Queen Wasp One is meant just for me. But hey! I have some
fantastic figgy friends...very fine they are too...in fact there
are exactly 749 of them. And each one is looking for their
special one-of-a-kind partner and some lovely pollinations.

—

Enter 749 singing and laughing different varieties of fig trees . . .

FIG TREES TWO to 750

Helloooooo you perfect 749 Queen Wasps. Wonderful to meet
you! How fabulous you all look. What do you say we pair up?
Get together. Let's all have a happy day.
We match up, you know. Isn't that fantastic!

QUEEN WASPS TWO to 750

Thoroughly delighted and giggling up a storm.
They each hover over their perfect match of a fig tree . . .

—

Oh! We love special matching figs. You all are looking
fantastic, too. Smelling amazing. Fig Tree One is right.
Mother Nature is great. She really does know what's what.

FIG TREE ONE

Excellent! That is exactly how things should be. Mother Nature
knows how to work things out. Let's see. Now Fig Tree 4,
you go with Queen Wasp 4. Good. And Fig Tree 359 you get
together with Queen Wasp 359. Fig Tree 750 with Queen
Wasp 750. That's it! And the rest…you know what to do.
Perfect, everyone. Now that's Mother Nature for you.
What do you say we get this pollination party started!

—

All Queen Wasps start to sing, OH HAPPY DAY.
All the figs laugh and join in . . .
Curtain falls to the merry buzz of figs and wasps
dancing, singing, and pollinating . . .

END OF PLAY

FOOTNOTE
The characters in this play are both a bit real and a bit of a theatrical
confection. For Mother Nature's truth is this. There are 750 species of
queen wasps in the world and 750 species of fig trees. And, amazingly,
each special queen wasp can only pollinate her matching, special, and
very perfect fig tree.

TREE'S STORY

ONE

when you think

once upon a time

consider me!

for who else still breathing
has been part of long ago
who else

holds it written in
rings of memory
for anyone to read
in the far future

but when I started out
don't imagine
I was much to look at
just one of a pale tangle of
timid saplings and yet . . .
somehow I survive

TWO

I am never alone
my forest family
a green-feathered canopy of
knowing trees protect me
teach me to thread my
roots deep into earth
to drink sun and water dots
through new leaves

I learn early the
art of tree signals
emitting secret scents
tiny currents that
send invaders flying or
call friends

in this way
as countless moons
parade silver
through night sky and
circled suns peep up orange
through distant earth cracks
I grow into my
true tree self

THREE

pulsing colored-hot
all sugared sap within
my roots surge faster
plunge deeper
branches turn
forever searching
sun drops
vapor mist
and yet—

crying silent like all trees
if I am
thirsty or hurt

creatures approach
shelter within my scales of bark
and sheer ribboned leaves
they curl inside my coils of fattened roots
while feathered things build
finely-twigged homes
soft-nesting between
my branches

humans come
sit near
admire me
tell me stories

for I am loved
and love back

and when I have flourished
my loud season of
leaves fruit flowers
I save green sun food
to sustain me for
the quiet times

FOUR

some years are hard

when unending waters

pound the ground

the wetness seeping far too close

to my heart

or when red heat unleashes

clouds of thick dust and flames

but even worse

when my wooded family

lose their places

are

no

more

and

me—

I weep as only a tree can
yet somehow I stay
feet anchored through
days and nights
of those many capricious
long agos

FIVE

it is then
I understand that I
a once timid sapling
am forever a part of
new canopies
new earthscapes

so
when you think

once upon a time

consider me!

for who else still breathing
keeps long ago alive
written in wood
stored in memory rings
for all the future

and while there are
clouds sun earth
a world shared
new rings will grow
new stories be told

for I am ever loved
and love back

THREE EARTH HAIKU

deep down
things happen
important things
yet how quiet
under my toes

hard-clumped
or soft-crumbled
somehow
always growing
one seed
or another

sing earth sing
I want to hear
grass grow
bluebells open
trees spring
sky high

THE MAGIC
HOUSE
OF SEEDS

once—
in the days when all things
grew and flourished
under
the brightest of bright suns
and rested under the
coolest of cool moons
each night—

50

there was a magic house
behind a great green door
in the greenest of green gardens
where seeds lived

51

not—
just a few seeds but
all the seeds of
all growing things
that ever breathed in
all the world

now—
each had been
soft-asleep since
that time when
everywhere
the sun shone yellow and bright
waters ran cold and blue and
earth sang rich and loud

and—
if you were to open the
great green door of that
magic house
step inside
listen

you could hear
the softer than soft pit-a-pat
of each tiny seed as it lay wrapped
snugger than snug in
crinkled cream paper
dreaming its
ancient growing dreams
pulsing its
ancient life

and yet it happened—
one terrible day
the darkest of dark
poisons came
spilling without a word
dripping without thought
flying without care
over earth sky and sea
and
earth could not now
sing joy

before long

trees flowers air and water

began to die

as poisoned darkness

spread into a lifeless

forever-night

covering far near and wide

thick

with mournful dust

however—

behind the green door

lived

the powerful wizard of growing things

who had been guarding that magic house

since

earth invented seeds

and

when the wizard saw the

poisons

he shed the greatest of great tears

knowing

the most terrible of terrible times

he hoped would never come

had come at last

at once he realized
earth had but one
hope—

the ancient magic
from those past days
when life breathed its first breath
must be summoned

the greatest of great wizards then
began to sing
that long-forgotten song of
earth and sky and sea

he sang until
he touched the
deepest of deep memories
longings and imaginings
of all humans who ever
loved a forest
smelled a blossom
or
sipped sweet water

the wizard ended his song—
but
the music played on
louder and longer
fuller and stronger
until at once
a mighty wind
fresh-born pure and free
blew open the great green door and
rushed inside the
magic house of seeds

awakened
by the trembling rush of
wilder than wild wind
sensing
the old magic —

one by one
seeds
popped from their paper beds and
rose on a breath up up up
weaving swags and circles
with the wind

till—
that greatest of great wizards
rose as well

together they soared
around the world
calling the old magic
singing the old song
chasing poisons
fighting dark

when at last—
all poisons
vanished
dust blew off

and earth breathed a
sigh
deeper than deep

next—
the wizard quickly planted
the perfect seeds to grow
perfect new forests and meadows
jungles and plains
     highlands lowlands
     wetlands drylands
     and on and on

as
air swelled trumpet-fresh
rain and sun streamed down
wet and bright with power
cracking open each seed
its
sprout-tender and
spiraling roots
springing to life—

until
earth
sang once again
and
all was joy

then—
as in earlier times
the wizard
gathered a seed from
each newest of new plants
wrapped it in
crinkled cream paper
and
placed it behind
that great green door
of the magic house of seeds

when at once—
that mighty wind
blew rushing and spinning
inside the magic house of seeds

'*wizard*'—
called the wind
gusting ever faster
ever bigger

'the poisons have returned
but your magic will not work
for today only
the smell of a blossom
love for a forest
taste of sweet water
can call forth the magic

and these
most human of human things
deepest of deep memories
longings and imaginings
are earth's true power
earth's true music'—

with that
the ancient first-breath of earth
mightiest of mighty winds
vanished

and now—

and now
only quiet thought
swept through
that magic house of seeds

the wizard
slow-understood

it is
humans
who must
summon the music
for only
humans
alive with earth's
deepest memories
longings and imaginings
could
call forth the power to
stop the poisons
vanquish the dust

but—
would they
dare they
remember the music
use their power

such questions hung
motionless in the air

and yet—
pulsing with hope
in the magic house of seeds
behind the great green door
in that greatest of great gardens
each seed
dreamed on
remembering
the taste of sweet water
heat of bright sun
and the
forever
rich and loud

songs of earth

THREE WATER HAIKU

hearing your trickle
I dream-float away
hearing your crash
hold   on   tight

falling
rolling
surging
like you do
ever wonder where
you might land

a quiet home
you make for fish
a fine place for me
to splash loud

BUG PARADE

When the bugs decided
to have a parade
ten quintillion came
who can guess what they weighed

Wings and antennae
went trembling a-shiver
while mini-legs scuffled
all directions a-quiver

It was just twilight time
not quite moon not quite sun
that cockeyed mad moment
beasties love to have fun

Off they went furrowing
jumping and burrowing
scampering scurrying
teeny specks hurrying

They whirred slid and squirmed
swam buzzed and turned
playing hooraying
batty bug holidaying

They whizzed by all zipping
glittering then flittering
diving and gliding
whoops sometimes colliding

Advancing while dancing
speeding receding
straying sashaying
wild buggy horseplaying

Teetering and skeetering
meetering and greetering
creepering and crawlering
a great insect ballering

But most bugs hate lines
there were ten quintillion whines
as they acted their worst
pouting, *I must go first*

Us us us called the **A**nts
we know the way
*we **have** to go first*
ant *starts with A*

What a loud babbling fuss
a bug rumpus and more
a million species spinning
a deafening uproar

At last they agreed
that the ants would proceed
with **B**umblebees busily
following their lead

Our turn next chirped the
Crickets
in an ear-splitting blast
no us snapped **D**ragonflies
as **E**arwigs crept past

Fireflies spun overhead
in a ring of bright lights
while **G**rasshoppers and
Horseflies
high-hopped in delight

Inchworms and June bugs
kept checking the time
as Katydids and Lacewings
squeaked *this row is mine*

Mosquitoes and Netwings
Owlflies Planthoppers
swooped about singing
every bug-tune showstopper

The Question Mark Butterflies
all orange and brown dots
claimed a row to themselves
joking *we deserve some good spots*

Rice Weevils and Stink Bugs
laughed as they twined
whooping *we love a parade*
as Termites crept behind

Underwings and Vine Borers
began to slow down
hurry up buzzed the Wasps
those *Xylodromumses are around*

At last came Yellow Mealworms
striped Zebra Butterflies
swarming wispy whirls
as moonbeams lit the sky

All bugs at last arrived
parading endless rows
when ten quintillion roared at once

***NOW* WHERE DOES WE GOES?**

COME ON DOWN TO FUNGI TOWN
A Wood-Wide-Web Rap

Come on down to
fungi town
see what's goin' on
way underground

Take a trip through earth
real brown
explore those f u n g i

m o v i n'

a l l   a r o u n d

They've got lots of names
not one the same
and spreading spores
their fungus game

They were born long ago
when nothin' else would grow
nothin' to see
not even one tree

But that time's long past
now they're unsurpassed
as they telecast
through an underneath

wild
dark
and
v a s t

They're impossible to know
go weavin'   to   and   fro
makin' webs of fine threads
keepin' every plant fed

And this universe below
you can't see with your eye
is secret and silent
like shooting stars in the sky

Because way down there
through infinite layers
spores have another pursuit
love seepin' into roots

Wigglin' through shoots
into anything that grows
for connecting all plants
is what spore fungus knows

They go
   criss-crossin' tangles
      wildin' wide in mangles
         reachin' far in gangles
            explorin' all the angles

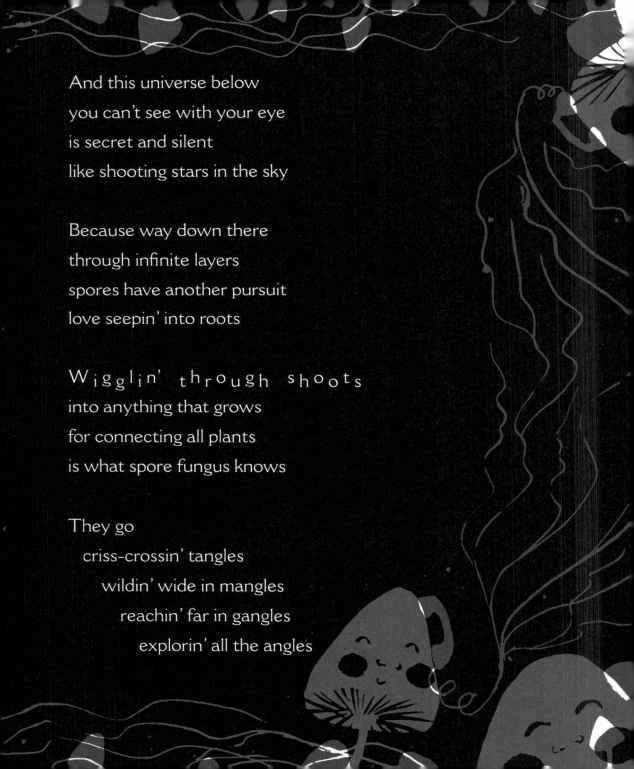

Soon every fungus spore
goes on linkin' even more
travellin'
door to door to door
till there's a labyrinth

beneath the sods and clods
of earth's wondrous floor

invisible
intertwining
indivisible
interlining

Then the whole understory
that giant dark inside
crusty moist and wide
hears the very same thing
like a telephone ring
a big group sing
or the racy call of spring

Shoutin'
Hey there oak
How ya doin' hedge
What's up elm
What's happenin' friend in
your house in this realm

Plants now all feeling great
learned how to relate
like a team of rooted mates
who would not hesitate
to help each other's fate

See when the going gets tough
they support one another
when things gets rough
they're like sister and brother

Now one thing's for sure
in this rap of under wood
fungi stay busy
doin' superhero good

And these microscopic beings
you can't even see
the ones who live under
every flower bush and tree
link all living things
one thread at a time

It's called the **wood-wide-web**
and it makes the world so fine

Cause fungi play their part
to keep the planet **strong**

So let's rock these superstars
think they'd really dig this song!

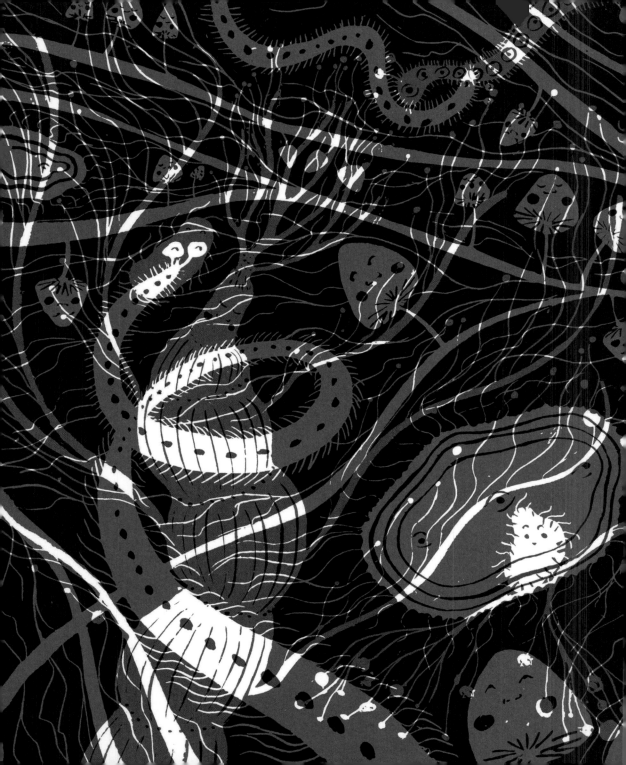

NIGHTINGALE'S STORY

ONE

day and night I travel
when I'm lucky
    wind carries me
but distances are great
cloud droplets quench my thirst
    my wings warm in yellow heat

      I cannot stop
      no one has told me
        but I know
      the way birds do
      to find a new home

          so I fly
            trees and mountains away
            fields and waters away

and in every
    head-turn sky-gaze
I understand
it's woods I seek
    things nettled and spiked
    rough-hewn brambles and scrub
alive in needle-sharp thorns
    barbed thickets
hidden low places where
    I can shelter
    find gentle safety

arriving at last
I discover my new home
    and inside that bristled
    hedgerow-tangle I rest
a brown-feathered ball
until I remember
    what I must do

TWO

for there are songs within me
     hundreds
I can sing them
     forward then backward
in any order

    rising on a flutter
       into end of day
    I alight on the perfect perch where
    obscured by twilight
       secure behind paper-thin new leaf
    I pause
      watch wait

     warm lemon-light soon fades
     lavender laces through darkening branches
     scents fatten

     it is time

my throat opens
I sing of me
of weathered bark and prickly brush
    against my chest
of soft-smelling grasses old leaves
    holding me as I sleep
I sing my ancestors

my music floods the night

    moonbeams soon twine
long shadow-braids
    through the wild wood canopy
distant hills rise higher playing
    dark harmonies of green and rock
quicksilver stars pop
    dust a-twirl
to my melodies
and all earth
shouts loud tonight

    with my song

THREE

I sing more

hit new notes

      bigger fuller

until

she

sees

me

I stop
at once I know
     the way birds do
she
is
home

and now

I will be safe

with this thought
     smiling snug inside
I remember my ode to spring
my throat opens again
for tonight
it is time to sing

the universe

I SPY

if I look deep
wide
far
I spy a million colors
sprinkling a billion shades
over the garden like
each had parachuted to earth
after this morning's big cloud shake or
popped out from the misty arch of
that surprise lunchtime rainbow or
sprung from the grass-glisten like
a trillion crayon dots
during this afternoon's noisy
sunbeam parade

but there's more

if I just wait till
wind scatters its blaze of
sunset-confetti over the
garden
then . . .

I can spy more colors
in more shades
than anyone could ever
sprinkle
scatter
or count

THE FAIRY GODMOTHER

A PLANETARY PLAY
(A Mother Nature Production)

Enter Fairy Godmother. She descends on a swing center stage.
In her right hand she holds a blossoming bough.
In her left she clutches a dead branch . . .

FAIRY GODMOTHER

Welcome friends
To this Planetary Play
Where creatures and plants
Will have their own way
And wish for such things
That please them each day
But to grant all these wishes
I must have my say
For all things on earth
Star in my play

ANT

Enters stage left carrying a marigold seed on his back which
is longer than him. Sees Fairy Godmother . . .

—

Oh, Fairy Godmother. I have a wish. I hope it's OK to ask.

FAIRY GODMOTHER

Of course, Ant. I would never
ignore you. You are too important to me.

ANT

Thank you. It's like this. I wish I had a lot a lot a lot of other
ant friends. Plus a mega-level, multi-chambered,
super-complicated cleaning colony underground.

FAIRY GODMOTHER

That is one long wish, Ant. But it shall be granted.
How clever and useful you are. And strong.

—

Ant goes off happy still carrying the marigold seed . . .

LADYBUG

Scuttles onto the stage . . .

—

Oh, Fairy Godmother. I have a wish, too. I wish for lots of
great-smelling meadows covered in merry wildflowers.

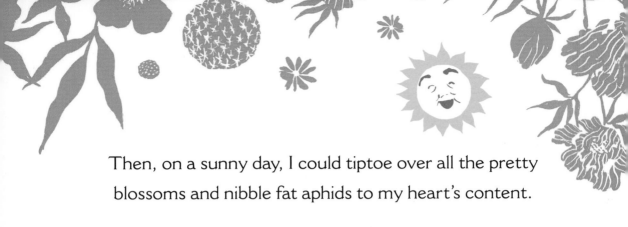

Then, on a sunny day, I could tiptoe over all the pretty
blossoms and nibble fat aphids to my heart's content.

FAIRY GODMOTHER

You too are important. But even though the humans have
taken away a lot of my meadows and wildflowers, don't worry.
I can still find some. Your wish is granted. By the way,
Ladybug, what lovely polka dots you have!
I think you look like a little wildflower yourself.

—

Ladybird giggles and goes off pleased as punch . . .

CATERPILLAR

*Enters . . . carried smoothly along by sixteen
hard-working little legs . . .*

—

Oh, Fairy Godmother, I wish I had a big fat juicy cabbage
that I could munch my way through.

FAIRY GODMOTHER

Of course. You are very special, Caterpillar, and here's the
good news: I still grow cabbages. Your wish is granted. Wait!
Before you go, know that I am looking forward to seeing
your dazzling butterfly wings when they emerge.

—

*Caterpillar goes off happy (and proud). He is excited thinking about
his new butterfly life where he gets to fly free with the wind . . .*

—

Now, is there anyone else who has an important wish?
I am taking all requests.

ALL THE CREATURES ON, IN, AND ABOVE EARTH

Crowding onto the stage . . .

—

OK. Our turn. Move over, brother. Sister! Watch your step.
Birds! Keep those wings folded. Hurry! Come on, everyone.
We don't have a lot of time out of water. Watch it, please. Don't
step on my hooves. Ouch! That's my paw. NO! It's mine . . .

They settle down at last . . .

—

We wish for endless food, good earth and sky,
and wild spaces where we can roam, swim, and fly.
Oh, and lots of perfect water and sweet-smelling air.

FAIRY GODMOTHER

Sighs . . .

—

Another excellent long list. But I don't know for sure about
that one. Wild spaces are pretty hard to find these days.
A lot have been used up. And I can't answer for the condition
of air and water. There have been some problems.
Humans, I'm afraid. Poisons.

CREATURES

What? Problems? Poisons? Why would humans do that?
They live here, too. We want our wishes. We need them so we
can grow and be bountiful and happy like we are meant to be.

—

Lots of frowning and anxious expressions . . .

FAIRY GODMOTHER

Don't be too upset. I will work on it. It gets harder and harder.
But I will keep trying. I promise you. You are not the only ones
who need all those things. The plants and trees and oceans
and rivers ask about it daily. They are incredibly demanding.
As they should be.

—

The creatures grow worried. They whisper anxiously to each other.
Just then all the plants and places on earth enter.
They crowd onto the stage . . .

ALL THE PLANTS AND PLACES ON EARTH

Hello, Fairy Godmother. Hello, creatures. You mentioned us.
Now then. We have a very big and very simple wish.
We wish we had see-through light, good soil, and clear water.
That way we can keep growing and flowing and generally
enrich earth and every creature on it. That means you.

—

Creatures smile and nod eagerly . . .

FAIRY GODMOTHER

That is definitely a good plan but a
tall order. However, maybe it will be possible
again one day soon. Stick with me. I will see if I can . . .

—

They all begin to say something but are interrupted . . .

ALL THE HUMANS OF THE WORLD

Our turn. Please. Just move to the back of the stage. Now then.
You know, Fairy Godmother, we really should have gone first.
We are the most important beings on the planet. Anyway, we
wish we had all of everything we need . . . and lots of things we
don't need. Just for the fun of it. It doesn't matter if we have too
much, we can just throw it away. Now this is important, Fairy
Godmother. We wish for a plentiful amount of good things to
eat and drink. Plus nice places to look at and play in. Oh.
And being quite sociable, we naturally wish we could be
friends with everything else on earth.

FAIRY GODMOTHER

Frowning . . .

Well, humans. If that is what you want, then stop fooling around with the planet. How can I grant wishes when you keep wasting what I have given you and interfering with my work?

—

She stops swinging. Holds up the dead branch . . .

—

I am warning you. You are getting in the way of Mother Nature. She needs her meadows back. Her wild spaces. And this continual wasting things is just not on. Plus. Her see-through light and water is very hard to find these days and well . . . she has a long list. You know what I am talking about, humans. Now pay attention. Poison is not a word anyone likes to hear.

—

Everyone and everything else on the crowded stage
gets upset at the poison word . . .

—

Mother Nature will not tolerate this situation with her earth. This disrespect. Other creatures and plants and places are as important as you.

HUMANS

What? Are you kidding? We are incredibly and extraordinarily
important in the scheme of things. We rule the roost.
But who in the world is this Mother Nature? Have we met her?

FAIRY GODMOTHER

She stands on the swing waving the dead branch . . .

—

It's me! I am Mother Nature. Watch your step. Do not imagine
for a second that you truly rule over anything. Or that you dare
to continue to get in my way. Remember. The only ruler here
is me. And Mother Nature always gets her own way. OR ELSE.

—

Lightning flashes . . . Thunder roars . . . The stage shakes . . .

HUMANS

Growing fearful and trying to run for cover . . .

—

Please stop. Please, Mother Nature.
We don't want an 'OR ELSE'.

Flashing light and noise and shaking subsides . . .

—

'OR ELSE' is too terrible to consider. We will try.
But the problem is, not all of us (and there are lots of us)
agree on the same things, Mother Nature. Still we promise.
We will really do our best to respect you.

—

Light, noise, and shaking starts again . . .

—

Please stop! Please! We want to live here forever with
everyone and everything else. We will try, as hard as
humans can possibly try, to get it right. After all,
we are the stars. The most important players on earth.
The most enlightened characters. The . . .

ANT

Marches forward quickly through the crowd still
carrying the seed. He turns toward the humans . . .

Knock it off, humans. You are not the stars of this play.
After all, there are far more of us ants than you. And all of us
put all together even weigh more than all of you put all together.
Therefore, logic would conclude that we are the stars.
Although the bumblebees always say they are the most
important creatures on earth. And then there are all
the earthworms who say . . .

HUMANS

Interrupting . . .

—

Ummmm. You have a point, Ant. Maybe it's all of us.
Maybe we are all in it together. Have a role to play.
Maybe we are all partners really. Best friends even . . .

—

Everyone looks at the humans. Then each other. And at last to
Fairy Godmother for an answer . . .

FAIRY GODMOTHER

Correct. You ARE all in it together. Each of you has an
important role. But most of all remember it is I, Mother Nature,
and I alone, who have the power to make wishes come true.
And by that I mean ALL WISHES.

—

Mother Nature leans closer . . .

—

Earth beings take heed
Do what you need
For wishes to be granted
Respect must be planted
OR ELSE
Mother Nature will
Have the very last say
In this extraordinary
Spin of a **Planetary Play**

—

Fairy Godmother waves her blossoming bough over earth.
Her swing rises steadily as a nightingale's hopeful
song fills the space . . . Curtain falls . . .

WHEN POEMS FALL FROM THE SKY

when poems fall from the sky

moon-dusted clouds

    draw swiftly aside

as earth and its creatures

    gather to hear

sea and its fish

    gather to see

poems afloat

a-toss without care

singing free
through waves of
sun-setting air
these
thought-dazzles flying in
shadow-glazed light

each of our dreams
adrift starry bright
as
all of earth's stories
soft-slide into night

and it's now
in this gloaming
my question uncurls
and it's now
in this twilight
my poem unfurls

how much longer
I ask
will we all be here
you and me
earth creatures and sea
to gather together
all under the sun
sharing stories as one
and how much longer
for I don't understand

will
poems
keep
falling?

SEED'S STORY

ONE

it has taken a long earth moment
all I had known was tight cold

    echoing stillness and the
    quieting of life
until in a cloud-shaking
    spring-soak
    tender-warm light

I crack open . . .
grow a root
soft-pulsing with hope
it pushes its way
    through moist soil
sucking porcelain-thin
    water
soon more roots come

they anchor me

    so march can't send me flying

they befriend the dark world of

micro-insects who go

racing invisible streaks inside soil

pressing deeper my roots swell

    till fat with confidence

they twine smooth system-tangles

    storing goodness

    shielding me from thoughtless poisons

and I . . .

know it is time

to grow up

TWO

a pale thread
    floss-thin with green life
cracks the other side of earth
my new stem strains surges to
      touch the sun
      brush the wind while the
blind planet-pull of moon
guards me at night

more stems follow
    stalks buds
    tight curled things unfold and
I surprise myself as
leaves flowers fruit burst into
a repeating festival of
shapes and colors
    which makes me
    me . . .

and in this heady moment
I open my eyes
    taste the blossomed air as
    rainbow water streams down to
    the tips of my roots
I hear birds
    breeze-tingling I join their songs
I play host to whisper-light butterflies
tease bees and wasps who visit

THREE

my life goes on happily
knowing I grow a great secret
for inside my flowers my fruit
    rest more seeds
    exactly like me . . .
which soon
    as the blue sky-umbrella folds away
    and warm sun slides to another place
drop to the ground or fly off
sail-spiralling unknown directions
    through chilled currents or

get carried toward the
blurred pale horizon by a medley of
shelter-seeking animals and birds

every seed now waiting
    silent unseen
until the next thrust of light and wet
knowing that tight cold
    echoing stillness
    and quieting of life
will pass
in just another
earth moment or two

COLOR HUNT

News Flash!

A host of new colors were spotted in the garden.
So I put on my polka-dot speckle-spotting shades
and went hunting for. . .

multicolor
technicolor
multi-spectrum
polychrome
freckliness
dappledness
stippledness
stripiness
spottiness
streakiness
rainbowness
wild-and-woolly

great big fat COLORS

When in two double blinks
Of sun's funny winks

I spotted
milky-white and burgundy
terracotta, ruby red
lily-white, lavender
turkey red, cherry red

I discovered
madder-brown and ivory
tangerine, mouse-white
citron, cadmium
alabaster silver-light

I tracked down
pearl-gray and smoke-gray
pumpkin, honey yellow
coffee-brown and sepia,
canary oh so mellow

I uncovered
strawberry, burnt ocher
myrtle, verdigris
moss-green and turquoise
pearly-white filigrees

I detected
amethyst and fuchsia
cornflower, mulberry
chartreuse and celadon
Alice blue dancing merry

I unmasked
saffron and emerald
king's yellow, old gold
tangerine, cobalt
cinnabar so super bold

I met with
inky-black, old ivory
saffron and puce
copper mandarin, olive
violet on the loose

But now I am bedazzled
bamboozled and bewitched
if I saw these all tomorrow
would I remember

WHICH

    WAS

        WHICH

THAT'S WHAT
FRIENDS ARE FOR

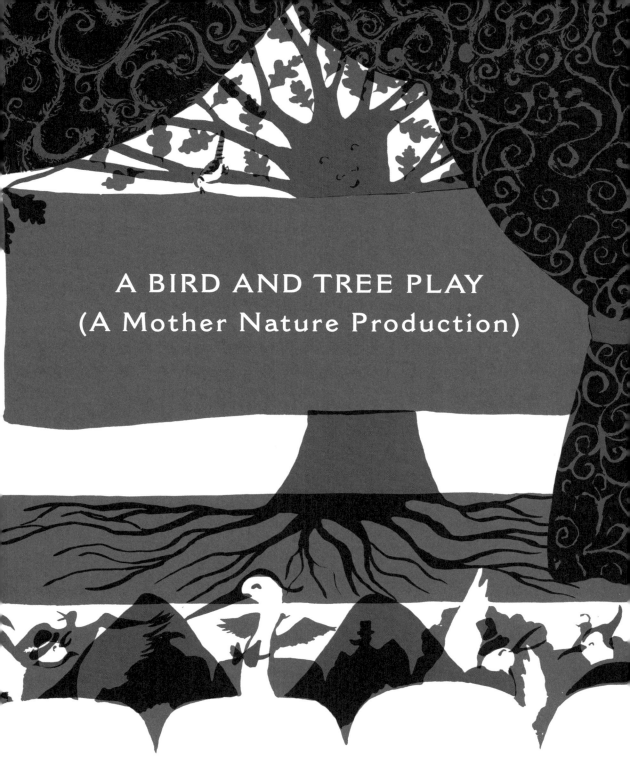

A BIRD AND TREE PLAY
(A Mother Nature Production)

Curtain rises on a country scene. Birdsong swells.
A great oak stands watch in the center of green
fields. All around him loud scents tangle with the hums,
buzzes, and chatter of intense plant and creature life.

Oak is happy. He sits watching the world go by. In fact he has seen
a lot of the world go by since he's been here for hundreds of years.
He is fat. Frothy with end-of-summer leaves.
He is admired and well-liked by everyone in the neighborhood.
Probably because he offers important things like food and housing.
Not to mention the kindness of his cooling shade in summer.

However, as autumn rolls over the fields, a few of Oak's leaves
turn bright yellow. Then some go orange. The changing
leaves make Oak think about his own survival.
And the future of all the other oaks.

In the midst of this seasonal reflection, a chattering dusky pink
bird with black and white stripes under its wings flaps its noisy
way onto one of Oak's many long branches . . .

OAK

Oh! Hello, Jay. Good to see you today. It's getting a bit cooler, don't you think. Weather is definitely shifting. I was just doing some big oak thinking. Mostly about next year. How about you? Are you getting ready to stock up for winter?

—

Smiles and shakes a few of his branches . . .

—

I bet you came for some of my wonderful acorns.

JAY

Settles down. Gets ready for a good chat with Oak. Jay uses three toes to clutch the branch in one direction. His fourth toe, pointing the other way, gives him a really firm grip. He could sit gossiping and chattering for days . . .

Chirp! Hiya, Oak. Nice to see you as well. No reason to get concerned about next year. I'm here to help out. I have been everywhere this morning. *Chirp!* On the move, Oak. *Chirp Chirp!* Always on the move. The hunt is on. And not a lot of days left. *Chirp!* Got to get settled in. Got to bury loads of food for winter.

Now then, let's talk acorns. Seriously. How many can you give me this season? You know I can carry six at a time. See, I use my throat and my long gullet, too. Clever, huh? No one else can do that, Oak. Not one of the other birds. Told you I could help out. But hold on. *Chirp!* I hope you are not thinking of giving any acorns to those pesky run-so-helter-skelter-all-over-your-branches squirrels. *Chirp! Chirp! Chirp!*

OAK

Yep. Pretty good acorn-gathering trick, Jay. You are one amazing bird. And don't worry. I am saving these just for you today. Not the squirrels. Now then, we will talk seriously about my acorns. I figure you could have around a thousand.

JAY

Feathers fluff in delight . . .

—

Thanks, Oak. A thousand! That is really great of you.
Stupendous! Awesome!

OAK

No problems, Jay. It works both ways. You see, I give you my
acorns. You take them all off somewhere. Bury them. Eat them
later when there's not a lot of food around. But since you can't
eat all of them, that means the acorns which are left over can
grow into new little oak trees in lots of exciting new spots.
And because of you, Jay, my future is assured.
There will be new me's. Oak trees forever!

JAY

Yep. *Chirp!* Totally understand. I'm a proud bird dad myself.
Chirp! Jay birds forever! *Chirp Chirp!* But really. Thinking
about it, Oak. Why can't you just drop your acorns and let
them grow up right under you? *Chirp! Chirp! Chirp!*

OAK

Simple. Oak saplings need light. Lots of light.
Tons of sun to grow into great leafy oak trees.
You see, a sapling would go light-hungry underneath
me and my huge crown of leaves. I mean, my little
acorn can't grow very well in my great big shadow.

JAY

Aha, Oak. I see the light.
Chirp Chirp Chirp!

—

Both laugh hard . . .

OAK

You are one funny bird, Jay. Great joke! But back to saplings.
Picture this. Say some of my acorns get carried off and are
buried by you. And say you don't eat them all, like we said.
Then, if no bears, deer, or pigs munch them up, and if Mother
Nature smiles on us, those acorns will grow up into new
little oak trees. And will get to plant their feet in a new home.
Meet new little creatures. And big ones. And me?

This is the best part, Jay. I get lots of beautiful oak children.
Breathes a big sigh of relief . . .

—

You know, it's always a pleasure working
with you. My future is looking much rosier.

JAY

Smiles. He flaps his wings hard. Chirps a lot . . .

Now I get it. Same here, Oak. I like working with you.
My future is looking rosier as well since my family will have your
scrumptious acorns to keep us going in winter. This is a totally
great relationship. *Chirp! Chirp! Chirp! Chirp! Chirp!*

OAK

You said it! Wish I could chirp myself.
(chuckles out loud)
That's what friends are for!
Thanks again, Jay. And good luck.

JAY

Jay laughs. He swoops down to the ground and hip-hopping along gets busy picking acorns up in his beak. He stores six in his throat and gullet. Then spreading his wings and lifting into the fresh autumnal air, he rises high above Oak's leafy crown of leaves. Up into the wild blue yonder . . .

—

You got it, Oak. Same to you. That IS what friends are for. What a view! Great color-spotting from up here. *CHIRP!* But hey. Don't move an inch, Oak. Promise? I'll be right back for the other nine hundred and ninety-four acorns in two shakes of a pesky squirrel's tail.

—

Big series of 'hahaha' chirps . . .

OAK

Smiling . . .

—

You're the best, Jay. Oh. Can't help myself here.
You are so funny! Hahahaha! I haven't moved for
four hundred years! Or laughed so hard . . .

—

*Every branch and leaf and even Oak's huge trunk, begins to shake
in unrestrained waves of giant tree laughter . . .*

*Curtain slowly falls to the whoosh of autumn wind, the rustling
and laughing of Oak's many leaves and the wonderfully soft
sound of a thousand acorns falling . . .*

WHEN LIGHT GOES A-DANCING

when light goes a-dancing

leaves go a-braiding all
green-laced and freckle-flecks

stones go a-bouncing all
twist-twined and jumpy-stripes

birds go a-soaring all
criss-crossed and polka dots

water goes a-flouncing all
gloss-swirled and sprinkle-sprays

clouds go a-puffing all
whisk-rolled and jumpropes

fish go a-swimming all
dappled-dots and spotty-slides

dark goes a-weaving all
star-popped and moon-specks

all day times
and
nightshines
and all times
and all times
and all times
and all
for
light is forever
a-dancing
with us all

THAT LAST SUMMER

they were everywhere
that last summer
rolling around her
muzzle
more scents
ricocheting unseen
through the great
hotness
of stand-still
August air
than all the fluttering
birdsong
in all the world
and of course—
she was there waiting
eager and anxious
determined to catch
every one

lying down
paws crossed
the way she always did
she sniffed
the violet-round
of ripening grapes
gliding like sugared
marbles
over her quiver-cold
nose
then carefully smelled
the heat-dried
once tender
sweet spring grasses
now hollowed-stiff
and sapless
tingling with
old musk

looking down
her nose twitched
at the strange
lemony scent of
countless tiny beasts
soft-scuttling
every which way
over the
hard-stubble earth
until she grew
distracted by the
rusty odor of
lichen ruffles
living their
paper-thin forevers
on the green oak trees

she gathered in
fresh cloud smells
of last night's
few drops of rain
while inhaling the
dripping spice red of
over-ripe tomatoes
clinging onto a tangle of
withering vines

she turned her head
as pale-yellow butterflies
circled by in wafts of
black-raspberry delight
and then followed
the intricate web of
minty breeze-trails left
by some end-of-season
rasping crickets

she caught
the fragrance of
coming fall in
the spreading rows of
gold-fattening pumpkins
and sneezed at the
scrubby lavender plants
after their mid-June
purple-fresh explosions

she considered
the candied rot of
last season's crinkled leaves
and savored the
sweet-sour long agos of
water-smoothed pebbles
resting motionless
under her

she knew
breakfast time
by the smell of orangeing sun
and dinner
by the silvering moon

and I am sure
she knew
the way she always did—

that this was her last day

as a distant dark wind
she had never met before
wound its smoky-cool
'come with me now'
scent
oh so gently
forever softly
over
her

AND SO IT'S FALL

and so it's fall

whooshing round the garden

calling yellows

signaling browns

soon everyone will

take off

I'm absolutely sure

IT'S ALL RIGHT

it's all right

we live the story of sunset
of sequined day and
moon-shadowed night
scented gardens
rock-fired mountains

we live the story of
a great before
of earthsea color and
sky-song

but
it's all right

yet how well we know
thunder's rage
the darkening of fruit

for remember
sunrise
is also our story
it just rests
soft now
before dawn

WE ARE FRIENDS

don't worry shadow
I'll be watching you
whenever I can
and
even if you slip under some
swish-darting fish or
w a g g l i n g tadpole or hide
under a lotus-pink lily pad
I promise to be there
when you surface again all
smiles
close to the water's top

and

even if you roll your jiggly spins

around those tall marshy grasses

I'll be watching

and

even if you carelessly bob along

chasing every dragonfly, water strider, and pond skater

you don't have to worry about a thing

I'll still be here when you finish

because I know

shadow

you would never leave me either…

wherever I am
no matter how
slippery you are

after all

we are friends

THREE MOON HAIKU

brightest bloom
in
night sky-garden
unfolding crescents

silver petals

now
wisp of quiet
breath

but not long ago

roar of a
dazzle-ball

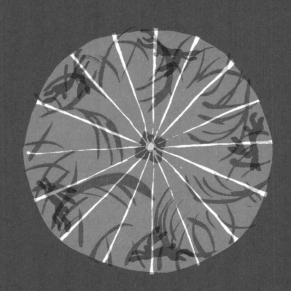

waiting for your
goodnight beams
to wrap me in
spangled drifts of
new dreams

Exploring some of the poems in more depth

This book is a perfect invitation for adults and children to talk about and engage in nature, language and poetry together. Here are some ideas for how to explore some of the poems together in fun and engaging ways, provided by the Centre for Literacy in Primary Education; an independent charity that works with primary schools around the country and beyond to support them in developing best practice in all aspects of literacy teaching.

CLPE

CENTRE FOR **LITERACY**
IN PRIMARY EDUCATION

. . . .

TELL ME SHADOW (PAGE 26)

Read and talk about the poem

Read the poem out loud together and discuss your initial impressions. *What did it make you think about? How did it make you feel? What made you feel this way?* Read it again, looking at how it is laid out on the page and what this might tell us about how to read it aloud. Think about the language that sticks in your mind. *What words, phrases and parts of the poem are most memorable? Why do you think this is? Is it the way the words sound? The images they create in your mind?* Talk together about the adjective phrases used to describe the shadow: *inky tattoo, a shape-changing / bobble-dark creature* as well as the verb phrases which describe how it behaves: *you wait / hovering and sun-silent / in some black riddle / of a place, bursting to plant / yourself into the / wide-open / anything-goes / light of day…, tangle up tall trees / fatten up lampposts / stretch passing / silhouettes / way / up / walls, lingering / raring*

to go / inside absolutely / e v e r y t h i n g. What do you already know about shadows? How do these descriptions fit with your experience? What do these phrases make you think or feel about the shadow? How do you think the 'I' character in the poem feels about the shadow? How do the illustrations add to your understanding of this?

Explore the concepts

Whenever the sun shines brightly, you can see the strong shadows it casts. Go outside on a sunny day, early in the morning, at noon and later in the afternoon. Stand in the same spot (ideally on a pavement or paving slabs), and find and see what happens to your shadow as time passes. If you have some, use chalk to draw around your shadow at different times of the day, marking the time at which each record

was made. The chalk will wash away next time it rains and won't damage the ground! Describe the shape and size of the shadow you see at different times and talk together about how the shadow changes at different times of the day. Look at the shadows cast when other objects block the sun's light and talk about their size, shape and position. Get a piece of paper and pencil and draw some of the objects you see and the shadows they cast. Now draw you. And your shadow. Everyone's shadow will be totally different and totally unique and wonderful. *How do the things you have seen and discussed link to the words and ideas you explored in the poem?* Re-read the poem together, talking about this in more detail.

Perform the poem

After you have observed and talked about shadows, and imagination read the poem again. This time, think about how you can perform it to enhance the meaning of the poem for someone else who is watching. *How will you use your voice in different ways to take on the intrigue of the 'I' character, questioning and painting a picture of the behaviours of the shadow?* Consider how to use your facial expressions and body movements to add to the storytelling, making sure these add too, but don't detract from the meaning of the words and the emotions evoked by the poem. You could record yourself performing and watch this back to consider the effect you have created and the impact of your performance as you watch.

Activate your imagination

Think about what elements of the natural world excite you, in the way the shadow does for the character in the poem. You might be in awe of a particular plant, insect or natural element. Take some time to gather all the ideas you have about this element on a blank sheet of paper; or get an adult to write these for you. This should be completely free writing and doesn't have to be neat. Empty your head of all the thoughts, ideas and questions you have, then look through your ideas and think about what might be good to work up into a poem of your own.

Come back to the poem on the page to look at how it has been shaped. Look at it, like a picture on the page. *Does the way it is set out remind you of anything? Does it relate to the subject matter?* Look at how the lines and verses are broken and consider the effect this has on how it is read. Have a go at drafting a poem of your own, thinking both about the words that you'll use and how they are set out.

BUG PARADE (PAGE 78)

Read and talk about the poem

Read the poem out loud together and discuss your initial impressions. *What did it make you think about? How did it make you feel? What were you picturing in your mind as you heard the words? What words painted these pictures for you?* Think about all the words that describe the movements of the bugs, like *furrowing, jumping, burrowing, scampering, scurrying, whirred, slid, squirmed.* Try acting out some of these out, discussing the similarities, nuances and differences in meaning of the words as you explore them through movement. Now, come back to look at the alphabetic list of bugs together. *Which bugs do you know? Which ones are new to you?* Use an encyclopedia or child-friendly search engine like Kiddle or Kidtopia to find images of the bugs and talk about these together. *What do you learn about them from the poem? What more can you find out about them from your own investigations? What do they look like? How do they move? What do they sound like? How do they behave?* Think about the way the bugs are introduced in alphabetical order. *Can you think of any alternative bugs for any of the letters? How would you describe these bugs if you were writing about them? What words would you choose and use to describe the way they look, move, sound and behave?*

Explore the concepts

Collect a notebook and a pencil and take a trip outside to a garden, park or woodland and hunt for bugs yourself. If you have a magnifying glass at home, take this with you too! If bugs aren't immediately visible, try lifting up rocks or logs, peer into cracks in tree bark, and look in long grass and on leaves. You could also take a piece of white cloth, such as an old sheet or pillow case, under a tree or bush and gently shake the branches. You'll be surprised how many tiny creatures fall out! Observe any bugs you find closely. Talk about whether you can identify and name the creatures you find, and how they look, move and behave. Listen carefully to hear if they make any sounds. Draw a sketch of them in your notebook, capturing their unique features and parts. If you don't know the name of them, use the sketches you make to see if you can match these in a bug guide in print or online to find out their names. *Did you find any of the bugs from the poem? Did they match with the thoughts you had about them when you read the poem?*

Perform the poem

As this is a long poem, choose your favourite part to perform. It might be the first part of the poem – building up the anticipation for the parade and moving into the different movements of the bugs, it might be the second part - naming and describing the behaviours of the specific bugs. Re-read the part you want to perform again, and think about how you might use your voice, your facial expressions and actions to bring the poem to life for an audience. Invite a friend or family member to watch you perform and watch their reactions as they listen to you.

Activate your imagination

Imagine you are an entomologist – this is a person who studies insects - and have discovered a brand new bug that has never been seen before! Close your eyes and picture your new discovery, thinking about all the features you observed in the bugs you found. *How big is it? What color is it? Is it patterned? What features does it have? How many legs does it have? Does it have wings? Does its body have different segments? Does it have antennae?* When you have a clear picture, start to think about how it might behave. *How does it move? Does it creep, crawl, squirm or fly? Does it make a sound? Where might you find it?* Now, take whatever art materials you have to hand and create a representation of your bug. You could draw, paint or make a collage of it, you could use recycled materials, specific craft materials or clay to craft a model of it. When you have created your bug, see if you can write a verse or poem about it, describing the bug and its behaviours, as you saw in the original poem. Display your art and writing together for your friends and family to enjoy!

I SPY (PAGE 100)

Read and talk about the poem

Read the poem out loud together and talk about it. *What do you think is it about? How does it make you feel? What makes you feel this way?* Look at the start of the poem together: *if I look deep / wide / far...* Look at the way the words are set out, how it slows down our reading to mirror how the 'I' in the poem is slowing down and looking more deeply. Consider the imagery in the poem. *What might this morning's big cloud shake represent? What do you picture when the poet talks about this afternoon's noisy / sunbeam parade? What might the blaze of sunset confetti, which the wind scatters over the garden be? What ideas do these things give you about the time of year? What season do you think it is? What makes you think this?*

Explore the concepts

Talk together about the differences between colors, tints, shades and tones. A tint is where an artist adds a color to white to create a lighter version of the color. A shade is where an artist adds black to a color to darken it down. A tone is where an artist adds grey to a color. If you have some at home, gather together some paints – poster, watercolor or acrylic – as well as some brushes and water, and explore and experiment with creating tints, shades and tones of different colors. Take the base color, then add differing amounts of white to create lighter and lighter tints. Now, take the starting base color and add differing amounts of black to create darker and darker shades. Now take black as a base color and add white in differing quantities to create different tints of grey, then mix the greys with the starting base color to create light and dark tones. Look at the range of tints, shades and tones you have created. Now, go out into the garden with your paints and try to capture the colors that you see. Use black, white and greys to create the really specific tints, shades and tones.

Perform the poem

Re-read the poem again. Discuss the feelings that the poem evokes in you. *How does it make you feel as you read? How does this compare with other poems like Bug Parade and My Shadow? Do you think you would perform it in the same way as those poems? How might it be different? Do you think this is a loud poem or a quiet poem; or does it vary? What makes you think this?* Re-read the poem and think about how you might use your voice, facial expressions and body language to create the feelings you felt while reading it for someone listening to you perform it. Practice a few times to perfect this. Consider how to use your facial expressions and body movements to add to the storytelling, making sure these add to, but don't detract from the meaning of the words and the emotions evoked by the poem. You could record yourself performing and watch this back to consider the effect you have created and the impact of your performance as you watch.

Activate your imagination

Take a notebook and pen or pencil and go outside. Take some time to observe and take in your surroundings. Consider what it means to look *deep, wide* and *far*, as it says in the poem. *As you look deeper, wider and further, what really captures your attention? What are the things you notice?* Note these things down in your notebook. Look for small details like in the poem. *What is the weather like, or what has it been like recently? How can you tell? What small details can you note in the environment? How do things move? What is happening with the light?* Keep adding to your notes, taking in more and more the longer you look. Come back to your notes and look at the things you've written down. *Can you think of some imaginative and playful ways to describe these things, like the morning's big cloud shake to describe the rainfall and the wind scatters its blaze of sunset-confetti over the garden to describe the leaves blowing in the breeze?*

WE ARE FRIENDS (PAGE 154)

Read and talk about the poem

Read the poem out loud together and talk about it. *What do you think is it about? How does it make you feel? What makes you feel this way?* Think about the title of the poem; *We Are Friends*. *What do you think it means to be friends? Who are your friends? What makes you friends?* Talk together about the friendship that you read about in the poem. *How do you know the character is friends with the shadow? What words and phrases show you that the character is the shadow's friend? How do they show the shadow that they look out for them and care for them?* Now look at the other perspective. *Why do you think the character has chosen to call the shadow their friend? What do they know about the shadow that is an important quality in a friend?*

Explore the concepts

Talk and think about how, in a friendship, each of the friends offers something to the other. In the poem, the character watches out for the shadow and promises to be there for it. *What do your friends offer to you? What do you think you offer to your friends?* The friend in this poem is the shadow. *Do you think you can be friends with a shadow? What do you think the character in the poem gains from being friends with the shadow? What do you think the shadow might gain from the friendship?* Now, go outside with a notebook and pencil and think about elements of nature you could become friends with. *What could it mean to be a friend with nature? What element of the natural world in particular might you be friends with?* Spend some time watching and observing this element of nature. It could be a plant, a creature, an element of the weather, or a natural phenomenon. You might choose to be friends with a sunbeam, a leaf, or a bee buzzing round the garden. As you watch your friend, think about what it looks like, and what it does. You could even try to draw it, to help you look really closely.

Perform the poem

Re-read the poem again, and think about how the character in the poem might speak to their friend, the shadow. *What sense are they trying to give the shadow? How might you bring this out in a performance? What tone might you use in your voice to reassure and comfort a friend? What volume would your voice take?* Look at where the lines in the poem break, and what this might tell you about how it should be performed. *Where might you take a pause? Where might you speed up? How might you use your voice to emphasise the meanings of certain words?* Practice reading the poem through a few times, trying out different ideas and then invite a friend or family member to listen to you perform it. *Did they get a sense of friendship and care from your performance?*

Activate your imagination

Come back to the natural element you thought you might be able to be friends with. *If you were to speak to it, what would you say?* Take a piece of paper and a pen and write down all your ideas of what you might say to your new friend. *How will you make them see how much you respect them and care for them? How will you show how much you have paid attention to them, to know how they behave and what they do?* When you have some ideas written down, see if you can use these to make your own poem, titled 'We Are Friends' about the element of nature you have chosen. You could also have a go at illustrating your poem. Look at the illustrations Junli Song has made to accompany the poems in this book for inspiration as well as the sketches you made.

ABOUT THE AUTHOR
AND ILLUSTRATOR

Zaro

ZARO WEIL lives in southern France with her husband, her two dogs, Spot Guevara Hero Dog and little Haiku, and a host of birds, insects, badgers, wild boars, crickets, donkeys, goats, hares, and loads more. She has been a lot of things; dancer, theater director, actress, poet, playwright, educator, quilt collector, historian, author, and publisher. Zaro's previous collections, *Firecrackers* and *Cherry Moon*, were widely praised and lauded for their brilliant wordsmithery and lyricism and their wonderful production and design.

Cherry Moon, illustrated by Junli Song, won the prestigious **CLiPPA Award** for outstanding children's poetry in 2020.

(Zaro's website: zaroweil.com)

JUNLI SONG studied economics and international development at the University of Chicago and then at the University of Oxford before radically changing course to study for an MA in Children's Book Illustration at Anglia Ruskin. On completion in 2018 she won a fellowship at Spudnik Press, a printmaking collective in her home town of Chicago, and is currently studying for a Master's in Fine Art. She previously illustrated Zaro's *Cherry Moon*, published in 2019 to wide acclaim for its brilliant and beautiful illustrations.

(Junli's website: www.artsofsong.com)

Junli